CONTENTS

INTRODUCTION

On visiting Buxton in 1783,
Georgiana, Duchess of Devonshire wrote to her mother, the Countess Spencer,

*'I never saw anything so magnificent as the Crescent
tho' it must half ruin me – my spirit makes me delight in the Duke doing it.'*

The Duke referred to was William Cavendish (1748–1811), the 5th Duke of Devonshire.

In 1780, he embarked on a project to create a fashionable, northern Georgian spa town to rival the spas in the south of England including Bath, Tunbridge Wells and Cheltenham.

The project, which focussed on the Crescent in Buxton, provided high quality accommodation together with bathing, shops and social amenities. The development, with its fine architecture and anticipated polite lifestyle, was designed to attract fashionable society. Given Buxton's remoteness, this was no small ambition. To reach it, visitors needed to cross the wilderness of the Peak District along roads that, at times, were water-logged, pot-holed and rutted. Some spas, particularly those closer to London, were patronised largely on account of a desire to socialise. Together with the fashionable, however, many visitors to Buxton were attracted specifically by the renowned therapeutic benefits of its natural thermal mineral waters. They came seeking relief from a range of ailments including gout and rheumatism.

Samuel Rayner, view of the Crescent from the Slopes (1851)

BUXTON BEFORE
THE EIGHTEENTH CENTURY

Buxton is situated over a geological fault. This separates carboniferous limestone, to the south and east in the White Peak, from the gritstone, to the north and west, in the Dark Peak.

It is from this fault that Buxton's mineral-rich water rises at a constant temperature 27.5°C. An early recognition of the value of thermal mineral waters was made by the Romans who established just two settlements in Britain with the prefix 'Aquae': Buxton, known as Aquae Arnemetiae; and

Bath, known as Aquae Sulis. After the Romans left, Buxton's thermal springs fell into relative obscurity. In the medieval period, however, Buxton's fortunes revived when St. Ann's Well became a site of pilgrimage renowned for its miracles.

During the Reformation of the sixteenth century, Henry VIII's chief minister, Thomas Cromwell (1485–1540), ordered the dismantling of the shrine at St. Ann's Well, so that, according to Sir William Bassett, *'there should be no more idolatry and superstition there used'*. Bassett reported, *'I have locked up and sealed the baths and wells at Buxton that none shall enter to wash there'* (1538).

Bassett's efforts were in vain. By the 1550s, the well and adjoining chapel had reopened. In 1553, the Cotterell family, owners of the site, were charged for allowing unruly behaviour.

In 1569, the Cotterells sold the well, chapel and surrounding land to George Talbot (1528–90), the 6th Earl of Shrewsbury.

John Speed's 1610 Map of Derbyshire showing the spring and the hall built by George Talbot and Bess of Hardwick

The sale was significant for the development of Buxton. The previous year, Shrewsbury became the fourth husband to Elizabeth Cavendish (1527–1608), better known as Bess of Hardwick. The marriage brought together two very important land-owning families. Shrewsbury and Bess set about creating facilities, including a generously appointed hall (part incorporated into today's Old Hall Hotel), in preparation for a visit by Mary, Queen of Scots (1542–87).

John Kay, 'Mary, Queen of Scots' from Hillard's 16th century painting (1791)

On the orders of Queen Elizabeth I (1533–1603), Mary was held captive in several properties owned by the Earl and Countess of Shrewsbury. Between 1573 and 1584, Mary made numerous visits to Buxton seeking relief from her rheumatism.

Despite the royal connection, however, Buxton remained little more than a village. The earliest known treatise on the medicinal benefits of Buxton's waters was published by Dr John Jones in 1572.

In the seventeenth century, Sir John Floyer (1649–1734) published a book on drinking water and bathing. He recommended Buxton's tepid and cold waters for ailments including gout, palsy, scurvy, leprosy and lameness.

Hidden Treasure

When the baths in the Crescent were renovated in 1975, builders found 232 Roman coins, 3 bronze bracelets and a wire clasp. This suggests that offerings were made here by the Romans to the Goddess Arnemetiae.

EIGHTEENTH CENTURY BUXTON

The CRESCENT, BUXTON.

Published April 20. 1796. by James Barkley, Buxton.

James Barkley, the Crescent, Buxton (1796)

Thanks to publications like Charles's Cotton's *'The Wonders of the Peak'* (1681), by the eighteenth century, Buxton's St. Ann's Well and nearby Poole's Cavern were tourist destinations.

Capitalising on this, and the fact that much of the land in and around Buxton was owned by the Cavendish family, William, the 5th Duke of Devonshire, saw the commercial opportunity to develop a fashionable Georgian spa. Existing visitor accommodation at the Hall catered for the elite and the inns in the Market Place for those of more modest means. To attract the true leaders of society, however, more opulent accommodation and facilities were necessary. This led the duke to appoint architect John Carr to design and oversee construction of the new building.

JOHN CARR OF YORK

Sir William Beechey, John Carr (1791)

John Carr (1723–1807) was born into a family of stonemasons and quarry owners at Horbury, near Wakefield in Yorkshire.

He was a prolific designer of country houses, prisons, courthouses, bridges, racecourse grandstands, town halls and hospitals. Apart from Buxton Crescent and Great Stables, his commissions included Tabley House, Cheshire; Harewood House, Yorkshire; Basildon Park, Berkshire; and the stables at Wentworth Woodhouse, Yorkshire. In later life, Carr suffered from chronic rheumatism. In 1775, he spent several weeks taking the waters.

In this definitive portrait of John Carr, Carr is posed with the plans and drawings of his successful project for Buxton Crescent. The distant view is of the spire of St Peter's, Horbury, the church Carr built in his native Yorkshire village.

Missing Plans

Although John Carr of York designed many buildings in Yorkshire, it is the plans of the Crescent (in Derbyshire) that he is shown holding in his portrait . He must have been very proud of the building! In recent times nobody has been able to find the original architectural plans of the Crescent.

BUILDING THE CRESCENT

Daniel Orme, the Crescent, Hall Bank, The Great Stables and St. John's Church (1837)

The choice of John Carr as architect for the duke's project was, in many ways, a natural one. Carr had already designed assembly rooms at Beverley in Yorkshire and at Newark–on–Trent Town Hall in Nottinghamshire.

He was also a director of the Assembly Rooms in York. In addition, Carr worked for the duke at Chatsworth House and Hardwick Hall in Derbyshire, and other members of the duke's family.

Politically, both the duke and Carr were ardent Whigs. Carr responded enthusiastically to his commission. An earlier, far larger plan, incorporating a fashionable crescent, was allegedly thwarted by the owner of a small, but necessary, parcel of land trying to capitalise on its pivotal position. Located near St. Ann's Well and the existing mineral baths, the Crescent we see today was the result of a second scheme.

The Crescent contained the St. Ann's Hotel at the west end and the Great Hotel and Assembly Rooms, containing the Ball Room and Card Room, at the east. In between were shops and six lodging houses. On the ground floor, the hotels, shops and lodging houses opened onto a piazza or covered arcade. As part of his commission, Carr also refurbished an existing suite of baths on an adjoining site for the use of gentlemen, ladies and the poor. In this way, the covered arcade linked the baths to the facilities of the Crescent.

In addition to the Crescent, Carr convinced the duke that visitors would be attracted by lavish and elaborate stabling provision. The octagonal Great Stables was the result. This provided stabling for 120 horses at ground floor level and accommodation for servants and artisans on the first floor. In bad weather, visitors to Buxton could enjoy the prospect of riding under a covered colonnade in the centre of the stables. An additional building provided facilities for sixty carriages.

Carr produced architectural designs in gothic and neo-classical styles, but he is most associated with Palladianism, the style adopted at Buxton.

The coat of arms of the Cavendish family in the centre of the Crescent (2024)

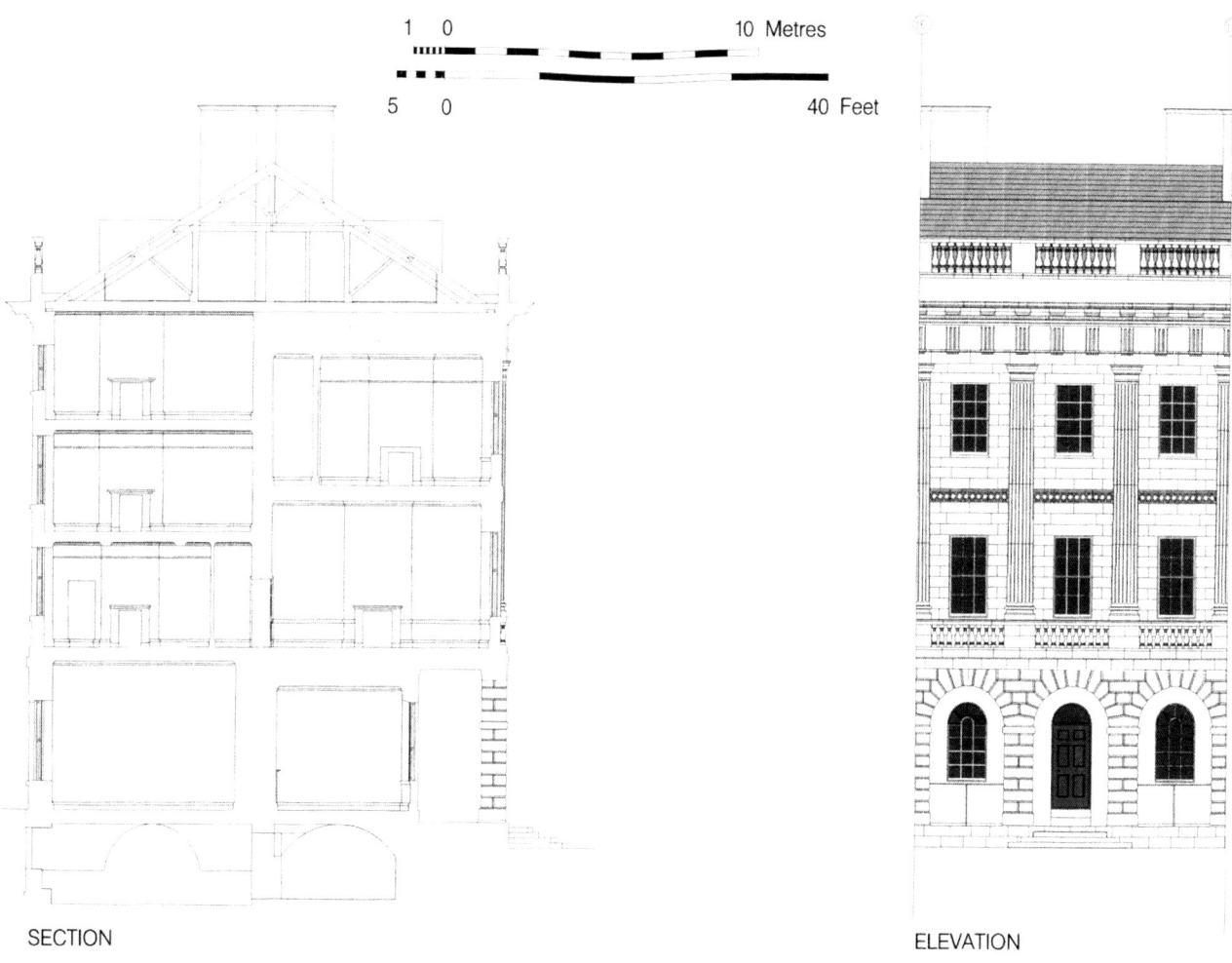

SECTION

ELEVATION

1   0   10 Metres

5   0   40 Feet

The Crescent. Cross section – showing extra floors of the front of the building;
Front elevation – showing the fine architectural detailing (circa 1970s)

This derived from the work of the Venetian architect Andrea Palladio (1508–80) which became fashionable in eighteenth-century Britain. It is based around classical principles of symmetry, harmony and hierarchical order. The Crescent is built on a semi-circular plan and differs from the more common elliptical plans of crescents found, for example, in Bath and Edinburgh.

Carr gave great consideration to the choice of stone for the building. Local quarries in Buxton and further afield in Derbyshire provided him with a wide selection of sandstones (gritstones) with varying properties to fit the task in hand.

The Crescent's front and side elevations are dominated by soaring Doric pilasters between the windows. The ground floor consists of large blocks of rusticated stonework. Above this is smooth ashlar stonework. In the centre are the arms of the Dukes of Devonshire, carved by Thomas Waterworth of Doncaster. They incorporate real stags' antlers, originally supplied from Chatsworth. Around the top of the building is a balustrade, a common feature of Carr's designs. The rear elevation is plainer with coursed, squared rubble stone replacing the smooth ashlar of the front. Nevertheless, it is still designed as a unified single entity.

Being in the centre of town and at the foot of a hill, the Crescent was designed to be seen 'in the round' rather than in the more traditional sense of having a public front and a private back as occurs at the Royal Crescent in Bath.

Before the building works started, some major engineering operations had to be completed. First, the River Wye, which ran through the site in a west–east direction, had to be diverted into a culvert further north so as to run behind the Crescent and, second, the main Manchester Road had to be diverted. Site work for the Crescent started in 1780 and took seven years. Construction took longer than expected on account of Buxton's cold climate. The building work was seasonal and all new wall tops were thatched for protection from frost when the site closed from November through to March.

John Carr's Horse-Riding Adventures

In 1795, at the age of 73, John Carr embarked on a long trip. He drove his own phaeton carriage pulled by a pair of horses. He wrote, 'the Open Carriage agrees best with me in which I travelled upwards of two thousand miles since the first of June.'

THE FINEST BUILDING IN DERBYSHIRE

The completion of the Crescent came at just the right time to take advantage of the rise in domestic tourism.

The French Revolution in 1789 and the onset of the Napoleonic Wars made European travel difficult. In response, the moneyed and the leisured who wished to travel had little choice but to tour Britain.

Despite Buxton's geographic remoteness, therefore, the Crescent was an immediate social and commercial success. Although there were some detractors, most contemporary commentators were dazzled by the building's opulence. Arthur Jewitt in his History of Buxton (1811), called it the 'finest building in Derbyshire'. Lists of people from the highest levels of society arriving in Buxton were published weekly in the Derby Mercury. The opening subscription list for the Assembly Rooms included the Duke and Duchess of Devonshire, the Earl of Shrewsbury, the Duke of Manchester, and the Archbishop of Canterbury.

The 5th Duke of Devonshire's total investment in Buxton was £63,218. For this he got the Crescent (£38,601), the Great Stables (£16,470), a remodelled baths complex and Grecian-styled.

The opening subscription list for the Assembly Rooms (1789)

Thomas Orde, Georgiana (1777)

William Cowen, view of the Crescent from the Slopes (circa 1850)

St. Ann's Well (£2,147), and the refurbishment of several inns and other properties (£6,000). By contemporary standards, this was quite an investment but one of the reasons why he was able to afford it was his ownership of the valuable Ecton copper mines in Staffordshire. The demand for copper had grown exponentially due to the practice of sheathing or 'copper bottoming' ships in the Royal Navy to protect their hulls and to enable them to sail faster. Between 1760 and 1790, the Ecton mine yielded a profit of nearly £300,000.

How Much?

Using the National Archives currency converter as a guide, the purchasing power in 1780 of £63,218 would have enabled you to buy either:

- *6,020 horses*
- *12,643 cows*
- *70,242 stones of wool*
- *11,110 quarters of wheat*
- *421, 453 days of wages for skilled tradespeople*

HOTELS, LODGING HOUSES AND SHOPS

In the eighteenth century, hotels were a new concept in Britain. Usually, travellers stayed at inns or, if particularly well–connected, in the local hall. The Grand Tour, however, provided the wealthy with the opportunity to explore the artistic and architectural wonders of Europe, especially in Italy.

While travelling abroad, tourists experienced 'hotels'. These provided premium accommodation incorporating a range of public rooms – libraries, smoking rooms, billiards rooms and coffee lounges – as well as bedrooms and dining rooms. The St. Ann's Hotel and the Great Hotel incorporated many of these features and were among the first hotels in the country outside London.

Daniel Orme, Portrait of Thomas Denman inside St. Ann's Hotel in the Crescent (1828)

Postcard of St. Ann's Hotel (after 1894)

St. Ann's Hotel remained in continual operation from 1786 until it closed in 1989. Its first proprietor, James Hall, moved to the Great Hotel and adjoining lodging house when they opened in 1788. The next tenant of the St. Ann's was George Goodwin. In 1811, Goodwin's widow, relinquished proprietorship to her brother Philip Moore.

Moore moved to the St. Ann's hotel from the adjacent lodging house and library. These were taken over by his son. The Moore family ran the St. Ann's Hotel until 1856 and, for a time in the 1840s, they also ran the Great Hotel. The business was then taken on by John and Rebecca Harrison who managed the St. Ann's Hotel until at least 1895.
Lodging Houses, synonymous with spas and resorts, including Buxton, provided an alternative to inns and hotels. Those in the Crescent were designed to reach the widest market possible by providing better quality rooms at the front of the building and relatively cheaper rooms at the back. To maximise the lettable space, an extra floor was squeezed in giving four floors at the back but only three at the front. The dining room provided the only communal facility in a lodging house and was located to the rear of the ground floor.

According to some accounts, the duke retained the middle house as his own town house. Newspaper advertisements, however, show that in June 1786 John Brandreth opened the centre house as lodgings for the 'Reception of Company'. Hannah Hodgson and Moses Muirhead operated two of the other lodging houses. From the start, therefore, the Crescent was given over entirely to hotels, lodging houses and shops. The Duke and Duchess of Devonshire stayed at the Crescent in December 1786 and January 1787 and frequented the mineral baths.

They returned for two brief visits in May 1788, but thereafter seem to have made little personal use of the Crescent's accommodation.

The Shops in the Crescent included a subscription library and newsroom, post office and what the Georgians referred to as petrifaction shops. These sold ornaments crafted from marble and the locally-quarried blue john mineral.

Isaac Cruikshank, The Lending Library (1800)

The Assembly Rooms' Ball Room (2023)

The Assembly Rooms were managed by the Great Hotel. They are the state rooms of the complex designed to be the most public and, therefore, the most sumptuous.

The Ball Room is the architectural highpoint of the Crescent. It is one of Carr's most successful designs in terms of its scale, proportion and detail. The room is seventy-six feet (23.16m) long, thirty wide (9.14m) and thirty high (9.14m). The decoration incorporates some of Carr's favourite architectural elements: a deep, coved ceiling, pairs of fluted columns with Corinthian capitals dividing the space, and pilasters lining the walls. Like the ballroom in Newark-on-Trent Town Hall, the room was influenced by the designs of Robert Adam (although he had no involvement) and by George Richardson's *Book of Ceilings*.

Panels of decoration in the ceiling are framed and deliberately varied in design. Carr brought his plasterer, James Henderson, from York to undertake this work.

Originally, the Assembly Rooms were furnished with sofas and card tables from Manchester. The chairs, marble chimneypieces and chandeliers came from London. The chimneypiece in the Card Room is carved from local limestone polished to reveal hundreds of fossils.

Assemblies were generally crowded with well-dressed people who danced, played cards, promenaded, or chatted together. Seating around the walls was provided for servants and for those too young, too old or too infirm to dance. The grandest assemblies started with minuets before moving on to country-dances. Formal events were called 'dress balls', and others 'undress balls'. There were also card assemblies.

Thomas Rowlandson, The Comforts of Bath:
The Assembly Ball (1798)

Thomas Rowlandson, A Gaming Table at Devonshire House, with Georgiana the Duchess of Devonshire (1791)

Secrets Behind The Symmetry

The two pairs of Corinthian columns, which appear to support the Ball Room ceiling are, in fact, constructed using non-load bearing timber. Even though they are hollow, they add symmetrical impact to the room and separate social areas from dancing areas. Two of the five sets of beautifully crafted inlaid mahogany doors, just lead to corner cupboards!

In Fashion

In the early nineteenth century women began to wear 'empire line' dresses. These had high waists and loose, flowing skirts draped to look like the dresses of Greek statues.

RULES OF
BUXTON ASSEMBLY ROOMS

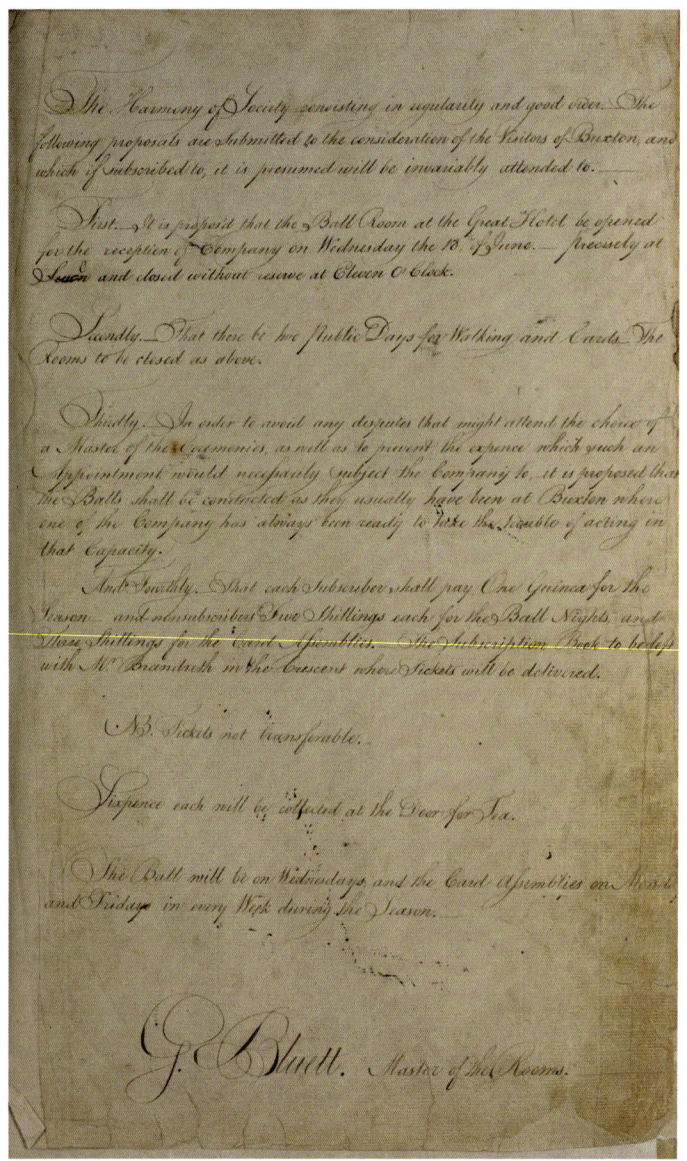

The rules for Buxton's Assembly Rooms (1788)

Following the lead set by Bath, assembly rooms across the country adopted various rules regarding management, conduct, dress and behaviour.

In 1788, the rules for Buxton's Assembly Rooms were written at the front of the subscription book by Gylbert Bluett, the short-lived master of the rooms. In charge of balls were masters of ceremonies appointed from among the subscribers. The Assembly Rooms were open from eight until eleven. Each subscriber paid one guinea for the season with their names written into the book. Non-subscribers paid five shillings a night. Two public days were allowed for promenading and cards. An additional fee of sixpence was payable on the door for tea.

Arthur Jewitt published an amended version of the rules in 1811, a copy of which was posted in the Ball Room. A minimum of twenty people had to have their names entered into the subscription book before the rooms opened. The one guinea charge for the season remained but the charge for non-subscribers was reduced to four shillings. Balls were held on Mondays, Wednesdays, and Fridays. On Sundays, tea was not permitted to be drunk, candles were not lit in the evenings and the Card Room was closed. A waiter at the Assembly Rooms kept the subscription book and administered tickets. Tickets were not transferable. Gloves were sold at the door for those who had forgotten them.

Fan with Buxton Crescent illustration (circa 1825)

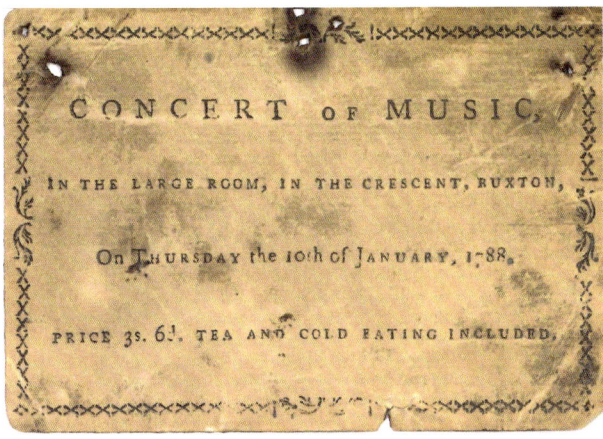

Concert of Music ticket, for the large room in the Crescent, Buxton (1788)

Fabulous Fans

Both woman and men used fans to keep cool, but also for flirting at parties and balls. People held their fan in different ways, using it like a code for sending messages. So, moving the fan across the cheek suggested, 'I love you' and closing the fan, 'I wish to speak with you!'

Last Minute Plans?

Did the Duke instruct John Carr to incorporate a Ball Room as a late design change? When studied closely, it does not fit very well into the overall plan and design of the building. The entrance leading to the Grand Staircase up to the Assembly Rooms, the most important entrance in the entire building, is the only one that does not neatly fit behind an arch.

Did You Know?

Music was hugely popular across Georgian Britain. Small groups of music-lovers gathered over the country, to perform concerts or just to enjoy singing simple tunes known as 'glees'.

ANNA SEWARD
VISITS THE ASSEMBLY ROOMS

Poet Anna Seward (1742–1809) was born in Eyam, Derbyshire. She lived in the Bishop's Palace in Lichfield, Staffordshire. Her circle included writer Samuel Johnson (1709–84), potter Josiah Wedgwood (1730–95), anti-slavery campaigner William Wilberforce (1759–1833) and polymath Dr Erasmus Darwin (1731–1802).

In the hope of alleviating her rheumatism, Miss Seward visited Buxton frequently, usually staying for a month on each occasion. She spent some of her time writing letters and observing what was happening in the Assembly Rooms.

In the company of Lady Harewood, she noted that in 1796, a Miss Mildred Lawley outshone all the other women present. In comparison to the other ladies who danced as though their legs had been tied together, Mildred Lawley seemed to 'tread in air'. One visitor, the 'enchanting Mr Erskine', honoured Miss Seward 'with frequent attentions in the ballroom', and with visits to her lodgings, where Erskine met 'the distinguished Mr Wilberforce'.

In August 1798, Anna Seward stayed at the St. Ann's Hotel. Buxton was crowded, but Miss Seward could not recall earlier occasions when 'so few families of rank' were present. Britain's war with France, she thought, had deprived Buxton of elegant young men. The only ones to be seen were 'a few prim parsons, and a few dancing doctors'. Nevertheless, she attended the Assembly Rooms with Lady Newcomine, and her three daughters.

ANNA SEWARD

Engraved by A. Cardon from the original picture painted in 1762 by Kettle in the possesion of Thomas White Esq. Lichfield.

Edinburgh Published by Mess.ʳˢ Constable & C.º March 1811

A. Cardon engraving from T. Kettle, Anna Seward (1811)

The Assembly Rooms' Ball Room ceiling detail (2024)

In 1808, a visit to the Assembly Rooms was interrupted by the arrival of the Marquis of Hartington and a few of his male friends. Miss Seward thought their behaviour insolent for failing to follow the established rules of the ball.

Poetic Prowess

At just three years old, Anna Seward could recite John Milton's poetry by heart! She was such a keen reader and talented writer that she impressed family friend, Erasmus Darwin, who encouraged her writing from a young age. Writing in 1796, Anna described the Crescent as 'a golden half-moon'.

TAKING THE WATERS AND THE SPA REGIMEN

Bathing and drinking Buxton's waters was part of the spa regimen – a series of activities prescribed by physicians. This included visiting the apothecary, gentle medications and eating a regular diet. Exercise, good company, rising early and the avoidance of business and study were also to be observed.

Dr Joseph Denman (1731–1812)

Joseph Denman's *'Observations on Buxton Waters'* (1793) noted that Buxton's mineral water was good for treating a host of conditions including: indigestion; acidity; flatulence; kidney, stomach and bowel complaints; a lack of appetite; and gout. He advised drinking two glasses of water before breakfast, noting their effects and adjusting the amount imbibed as appropriate. Denman thought some patients would benefit from adding a few drops of tincture of cardamom to the water. In addition, he recommended bathing between breakfast and dinner in tepid water.

Bathing with clothes on!

Despite the popularity of spa towns during the Georgian period, it was commonly believed that bathing was unhealthy as soaking in water, and especially hot water, was thought to let disease enter the body. When Georgians did take a bath, they would therefore do so without removing all their clothes – a habit that remained until the end of the nineteenth century.

St. Ann's Well, designed by John Carr and completed in 1783.

ST ANN'S WELL Buxton

A COURSE IN THE WATERS:
LORD & LADY MACARTNEY VISIT BUXTON

Lord and Lady Macartney stayed in Buxton in 1789 and 1790. Their route from London took them through Barnet, Kettering, Loughborough, Derby and Ashbourne.

George Macartney (1737–1806) was a career diplomat with postings in Cape Colony, China, India, Italy, Russia and the West Indies. Jane Macartney (1742–1828) was the daughter of the third Earl of Bute and Prime Minister (1762–63). The Macartneys travelled in a barouche, a four-wheeled carriage, accompanied by their servants. The final stage of their journey to Buxton from Ashbourne required seven horses. In 1790, their accommodation at the Great Hotel in the Crescent included two bedrooms and a drawing room, bedrooms each for a lady's maid and a valet, and two additional bedrooms for their four other servants.

In a letter to Sir George Staunton in 1789, Lord Macartney explained that he had gone to Buxton 'for a course in the waters'. Macartney suffered from gout and rheumatism and had been wounded in a duel. Assisted by an attendant, he bathed daily in the Gentlemen's Bath, visited the doctor and the apothecary. The Macartneys drank from St. Ann's Well and gave the well women 10s 6d. The Macartneys visited Castleton and Kedleston Hall in Derbyshire, Ilam in Staffordshire, and Lyme Park in Cheshire. All, except Lyme Park, were popular tourist destinations.

Aside from the money spent on taking the waters, the Macartneys subscribed to the Assembly Rooms and made charitable donations enabling the poor to bathe. At Buxton's theatre in 1790, Richard Brinsley Sheridan's play *The Rivals* was performed 'by the desire of Lord and Lady Macartney'. Lady Macartney bought tickets for their servants to see the production. In addition to their accommodation, food and drink, they paid for candles, coal and laundry. Payments to a blacksmith, stable boy, saddler, chambermaid, shoe cleaner, and for a servant to wait on the Macartneys servants show the range of services required to ensure that the spa resort ran smoothly. Revealing the variety of goods available to Buxton's wealthy Georgian visitors, the Macartneys purchased inkstands, a backgammon board, a purse, gloves, millinery, books, hair powder, and petrifactions made from blue john.

Visitors like the Macartneys spent their days taking the waters, promenading, catching up on events in the newsroom, borrowing books from the circulating library in the Crescent, writing letters and paying social calls. The more adventurous made excursions to tourist attractions including Poole's Cavern and Dovedale, went riding, hunting or to the races in Fairfield. Evenings were spent at the theatre and concerts, playing cards or attending balls in the Assembly Rooms.

WELL WOMEN AND SERVANTS IN BUXTON

Daniel Orme, Martha Norton, Well Woman of Buxton aged 91 (1820)

Well Women

Each year Buxton's parish vestry elected well women from among the poor. They assisted visitors and received gratuities instead of pay. Between 1775 and 1820, Martha Norton was elected fifteen times to the position. Their duties included serving water to visitors, cleaning the charity baths, helping the poor in the baths and drying linen. Well women gained public recognition. In old age, Martha Norton was sketched on at least four occasions. Engravings of her image could be purchased at the post office in the Crescent.

George Romney, 'Lady Hester Newdigate' (1790)

Servants in Georgian Buxton

No elite member of society would have contemplated arriving at a spa resort without at least one servant. In 1799, the Hon. Sarah Murray of Kensington advised that when staying in one of Buxton's hotels, the presence of a male servant was useful if for no other reason than to have a footman 'wait upon you at table'. If finances permitted or if you wished to make a show, more servants did not go unnoticed by fellow visitors. In 1781, the arrival of the Edmonstone family prompted Lady Hester Newdigate (1737–1800) to comment on their splendid coach and four, their many footmen and other servants in and out of livery. On other occasions she wrote about the arrival of fine coaches and of her disappointment if their occupants were not people of consequence. The presence of servants in Buxton is noted in correspondence and journals. Unlike Lady Jane Macartney's lady's maid, Jane Spencer, and Lord Macartney's valet, Russell, however, few are known by name.

Practical Pockets

In an age before handbags, women used pockets to carry their personal possessions underneath their skirts. These were deep cloth bags which were completely separate from a woman's dress. Objects that might be found in a pocket included money, letters, a journal, a handkerchief, a pair of scissors, a comb, writing implements, keys, a watch, glasses, a snuffbox, smelling salts, food and sewing accessories.

The St. Ann's Cliff, opposite the Crescent, was landscaped by Jeffry Wyatt in 1818 to create promenade walks

A Lady's Maid

Publications like Samuel and Sarah Adams's '*The Complete Servant*' (1825) set out the duties expected of servants. A lady's maid should be neat and clean in both appearance and dress. She should have good manners, be adept at needlework and be punctual. She was to take care of her mistress's wardrobe, to check clothing after it had been worn, repair any damage and remove dirt or stains. Each day, a lady's maid set out the clothes required by her mistress for the morning and ensured that hot water was available for washing. She combed her mistress's hair and attended her while dressing. Afterwards, she made sure the room was tidy, undertook any dressmaking and millinery work as instructed and laid out a change of clothes for the afternoon or evening. She helped her mistress dress for dinner or an evening out and undress before retiring for the night. If her employer was elderly, infirm or ill (as many visitors to Buxton were), a lady's maid might be required to sit with her mistress, read to her or administer medicines.

A Valet

A gentleman's personal needs were attended to by his valet. He waited upon his master when dressing and cared for his clothing. He ensured that fires were laid and that the washstand had clean water, towels, brushes and shaving equipment. In preparation for use, razors, warmed in water, were dried and then polished on a strop. If the master returned home wet, for example, from riding (a regular activity undertaken in Buxton), it was the valet's responsibility to provide warm, dry clothing, and remove the wet clothes for drying, cleaning and airing.If staying at an inn or a hotel, it was the valet's responsibility to ensure that all his master's luggage was carried to his rooms. If there was no footman in attendance, the valet also had to make any below stairs arrangements and wait at table.

The popularity of Buxton's waters attracted all ranks of society. Water from St. Ann's Well was freely available but charitable access to the baths for the poor was not so easy.

In 1597, parliament passed a law forbidding begging at Buxton and Bath. The poor who came in search of a water cure needed passes signed and dated by two magistrates.

In the early-eighteenth century, the ill and impotent poor who came to Buxton were generally treated as beggars and could be forcibly removed. The cost of looking after the poor from outside the parish was not the responsibility of Buxton's residents. This situation, however, did not mean that the poor received no help.

William Martin, St. Ann's Well (1796)

In the late-eighteenth century, the poor had the use of an open air bath fed from the overflow of the gentlemen's bath. The poor bath measured seventeen feet (5.18m) by ten (3m) and was five feet four inches (1.63m) deep. In the 1790s, Dr Denman noted that until lately the poor bath was 'shamefully and unwarrantably neglected, and in great disorder'. When bathing facilities were improved in the 1780s, the poor bath was sited further away from the gentlemen's bath. This new bath measured eight feet square. Like its predecessor, water came from the gentlemen's bath.

Treating the Poor

'The poor at their bath are not only exempted from all charge, but also meet with great assistance and support from the charitable company, who resort to Buxton,' declared James Pilkington in 1789. Treating the poor was possible because of the way in which the money used to support them was raised. From the later-eighteenth century, each visitor staying overnight in a hotel or lodging house contributed a shilling towards medical assistance for the poor. The money was collected by a steward. As the amount of accommodation increased and more visitors arrived, the amount collected also increased. This sum was augmented by money collected during two special sermons each year.

C. Hutchins, 'Please to Bestow Your Charity on the Buxton Baths' (circa 1840s)

Although the poor had access to medical assistance, medicines and the baths, conditions were attached. In 1785, poor people living within a seven mile (11.3km) radius of Buxton had no recourse to the charity. Financial assistance was provided between May and October only to a maximum of sixteen people at any given point.

Potential recipients of relief had to apply in writing and, if accepted, had to produce the response of the charity's treasurer on arrival. They also had to have the written support of a respectable person stating that they were worthy individuals.

The money and management of the poor was administered by a committee. It became known as the Buxton Bath Charity. One hundred and fifty people were treated in 1811; a figure that rose to 600 annually in the mid–1820s.

Each poor person received an allowance of up to six shillings a week for a maximum of five weeks. An additional four shillings could be allocated to those most in need.

Supporters of applications committed themselves to paying for any expenses in the event that the poor person died in Buxton, Fairfield, or on their return journey. Paupers had to supply documentation from their parish stating their place of settlement and medical certificates confirming that Buxton's waters would be of benefit. Those in receipt of assistance were not allowed to beg or accept any other charity while in Buxton. Allowances were stopped for any recipient found swearing, drunk or misbehaving.

Augustus Bozzi Granville's Observations

Alexander Craig, Augustus Bozzi Granville (date unknown)

Physician Augustus Bozzi Granville (1783–1872) was born in Milan, practised medicine across Europe, joined the Royal Navy and eventually settled in London. He was an authority on German spas. In 1841, he published an account of English spas and sea–bathing places and had much to say about Buxton.

In the dim light of the public baths, Granville thought the water 'dingy and greenish'. He observed a 'pot–bellied farmer of sixty, half–palsied', a lame artisan with calloused hands, and many others suffering from skin disorders; all plunging into the water. Some scrubbed their skin with a hand brush provided for the purpose. When the sun shone through the windows, he saw a layer of scum covering the water. An attendant occasionally swept the surface with a broom, but all this appeared to do was to mix the scum with the rest of the water. Granville was not tempted to join them.

BATHING.

Poor Bath, engraving from 'The Water Cure Illustrated' (1870)

The Gentlemen's Bath at Buxton (circa early 1800s)

Granville related the tale of two men, one an officer in the Life Guards, who agreed to go to the public bath early one morning in the hope of avoiding the crowds. In the murky light they could see no one else. On raising his head from the water, however, the Life Guard came face-to-face with his tailor from Chester who greeted him with the words, 'How do you do, Sir Richard?' Granville had no hesitation about bathing when it came to the gentlemen's private bath.

Here the water was 'a beautiful transparent light emerald-green colour'. Using the steps, Granville made a gradual entry into the water. The cold took his breath away.

He retreated and then plunged in, staying for about ten minutes. He got out, then went into the water for a third time. From his experiment, he concluded that the best way of using the baths was 'not to plunge, but to walk gradually and quickly into the water up to the chin', and out of it as quickly. He recommended repeating the process several times before taking a 'real bath'.

THE LOUNGE & LIFT, CRESCENT HOTEL, BUXTON
C J Smitter proprietor

The lounge and lift, Crescent Hotel, formerly the Great Hotel (post 1905)

James Hall was the tenant of the Great Hotel for twenty–one years until his death in 1808.

Hall's widow ran the business for the next eight years with the assistance of her nephew, James Muirhead. After 1816, Muirhead managed the hotel alone until he was declared bankrupt in 1833. By then, he owed £4,000 to the Duke of Devonshire.

Music for the soul

In August of 1824 Anne Lister visited Buxton. She stayed seven weeks whilst her aunt, who suffered from rheumatism, took the water treatments. She records in her diary how she listened to the duke's band which played in the Crescent usually between 11 am and noon. She mentions that the music provoked sad memories and on another occasion that it made her muse upon a love affair.

Dining Room, Crescent Hotel (post 1905)

The Great Hotel's next proprietors included William Shaw and Philip Moore. Augustus Bozzi Granville reported in 1840, that 'A lady, her maid and two menservants will be charged a guinea a day at the Great Hotel whereas the same number of persons, it is supposed, could be boarded well for three pounds a week at a respectable lodging house'.

True or False?

Adverts for the Crescent Hotel hailed the "Magnificent Adam Dining Room – the finest in the Kingdom". But this wasn't entirely true! The design of the plasterwork was inspired by Robert Adam a fashionable Georgian architect, but John Carr designed it and brought his plasterer, James Henderson, from York to do the job.

Edward Hancock became the proprietor of the Great Hotel in 1847. The following year, however, the hotel closed and was divided into three boarding and lodging houses. One, including the Assembly Rooms, was run by William Hicklin; another by Hannah Gregory and another by John Smilter. The Assembly Rooms continued to host balls and promenades each week. The boarding and lodging houses remained in operation for the next twenty years until Smilter reunited the houses and re-opened the Great Hotel as the Crescent Hotel. It continued as a family-run enterprise until the death of John Christopher Smilter in 1934.

The Crescent Hotel (circa 1910s)

Bates' views of Derbyshire: The Old Hall, Buxton (circa 1870)

Throughout the Georgian period and the first half of the nineteenth century, the remoteness of Buxton ensured a small and self-selecting market for the spa.

This led to a perception that Buxton was an exclusive place and, for many, that was an important part of its attraction. The reality, however, was that Buxton also relied on the presence of middle-rank visitors.

This became clear in 1812. Fear of Luddite rioters destroying textile machinery prevented many of the merchants and mill owners in the Lancashire and Yorkshire textile districts from leaving their homes and premises.

The Duke of Devonshire's agent reported that Buxton was empty. Only the Great Hotel, commandeered as the headquarters of General Thomas Maitland's troops, was occupied. The end of the Napoleonic Wars in 1815 brought an economic depression. This was made worse by a financial crisis in the mid-1820s. The effects of these national events were felt in Buxton. By 1828, the hotels in the Crescent and the Hall Hotel owed a combined rent of more than £7,000 to William Cavendish (1790–1858), the 6th Duke of Devonshire. He wrote off the debts.

Changes in the Crescent's fortunes appear to mirror the faltering of other inland spa resorts. This is often attributed to competition from seaside resorts, the popularity of European spas following the Napoleonic Wars, and the retreat of the elite from public spaces like assembly rooms. In Buxton, balls and promenades continued, but a shrinking number of subscribers to the Assembly Rooms brought an end to the recording of names in the subscription book in 1840.

Undoubtedly, the hotels in and around the Crescent endured a difficult period in the 1820s, but their temporary difficulties have overshadowed significant investment in the town under the Dukes of Devonshire following the completion of the Crescent. The construction of lodging houses on Hall Bank (1792–98) and the Square (1806–7) was followed by the consecration of St John's church (1812). There were alterations to the Natural Baths between 1803 and 1806. The landscaping of the Slopes opposite the Crescent by leading architect and landscape designer Jeffry Wyatt (1766–1840) in 1818 was followed by the provision of spring water to the Hall Hotel and the Crescent in 1820.

Despite these developments, renewed interpretations of the value of water cures and a growing emphasis on specialist treatments by the likes of Sir Charles Scudamore, meant that Buxton required new investment and a change in direction. Nevertheless, they provided solid foundations upon which Buxton's growth in the second half of the nineteenth century could build.

Much needed change in Buxton came in 1863 with the arrival of two railway lines; one from Manchester and the other from London via Derby and the picturesque Peak District. They proved to be of immense importance. The town became accessible for day-trippers and longer-stay visitors from the rapidly expanding towns and cities of Lancashire, Yorkshire, Staffordshire, and beyond. The railways acted as a catalyst for further growth with a vast building programme of hotels, lodging houses, speculative housing, and retirement villas.

Marketing itself as 'The Mountain Spa,' Buxton's visitors were entertained in the new Pavilion Gardens, which opened in 1871 complete with a concert hall, glazed winter gardens, a boating lake, tennis courts, and an ice rink. The Opera House, designed by renowned theatre architect Frank Matcham, opened in 1903.

Engraver Newman J. and Co. Panoramic view of Buxton, with the North West and Midland railway stations visible in the top right (circa 1870s)

LEE WOOD HOTEL.   CORBAR.

HE PAVILION & GARDENS.   ST JOHN'S CHURCH.   OLD HALL HOTEL.   HOSPITAL   ST ANN'S HOTEL.   CRE
NATURAL BATHS.
GEORGE HOTEL.

Panoramic

LMS
BUXTON
THE MOUNTAIN SPA
BY S.J.LAMORNA BIRCH. R.W.S.

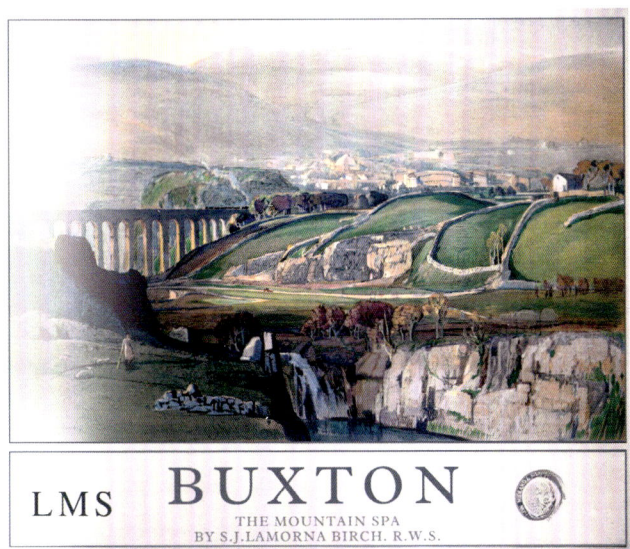

S.J. Lamorna Birch R.W.S, London Midlands Scottish Railway poster for Buxton The Mountain Spa (1924)

BUXTON

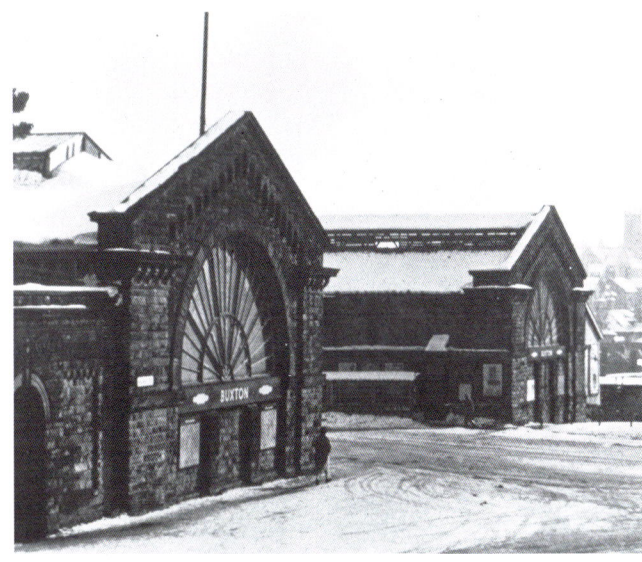

Two Buxton Railway Stations, Station Road, Buxton (circa 1960s)

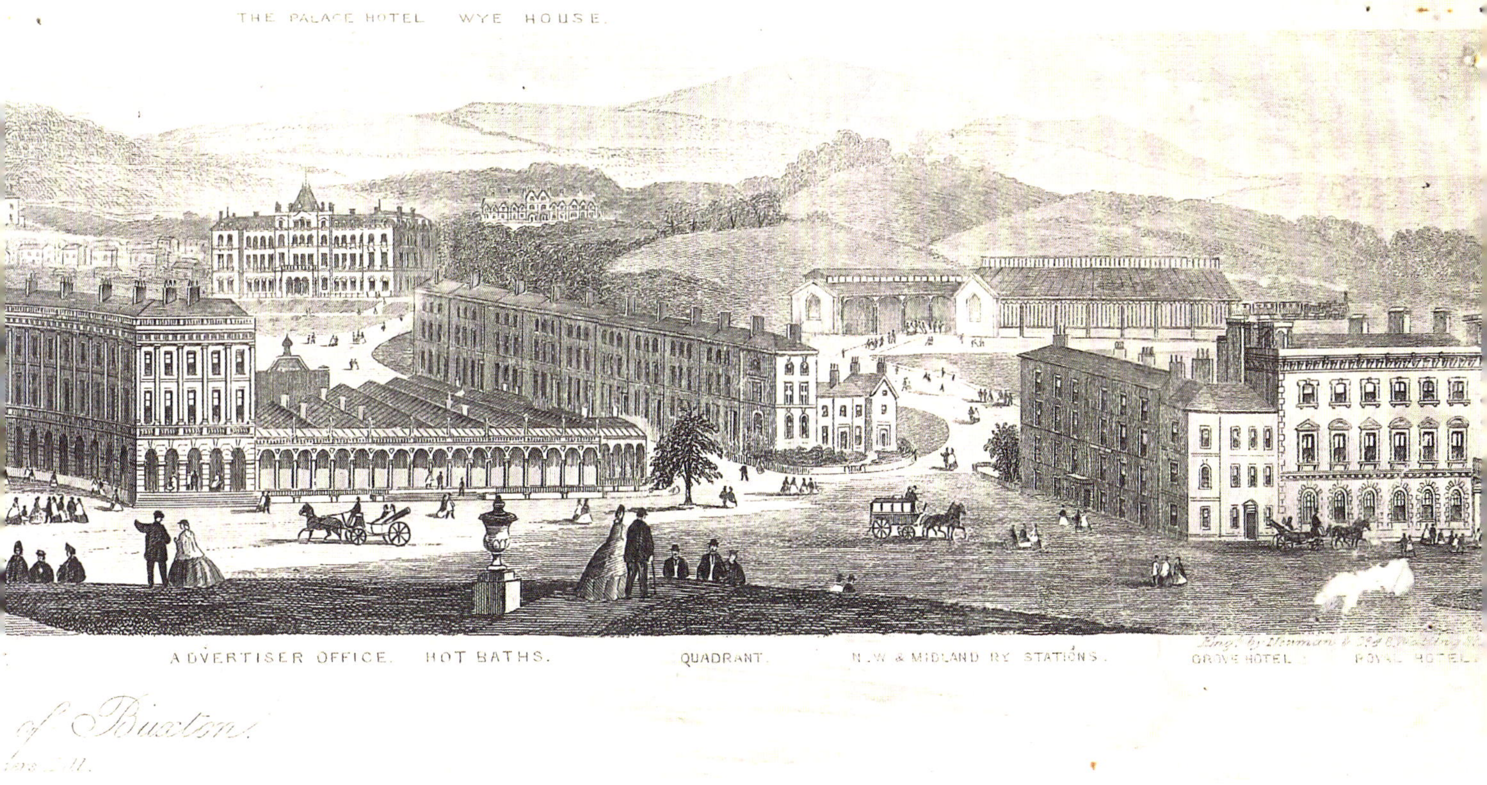
THE PALACE HOTEL
WYE HOUSE.
ADVERTISER OFFICE.
HOT BATHS.
QUADRANT.
N.W. & MIDLAND RY. STATIONS.
GROVE HOTEL
ROYAL HOTEL
of Buxton.

BUXTON AS A CENTRE FOR HYDROTHERAPY

112   **HYDROPATHICS.**

BUXTON HYDRO,

BUXTON (Derbyshire).

HIGH-CLASS HEALTH & PLEASURE RESORT.

260   ROOMS.

EXCELLENT CUISINE.   LUXURY WITH ECONOMY.

Hydropathic and Electric Baths of every description.

Schnee Bath and the Nauheim Treatment for the Heart.

Overlooking Gardens, near Golf Links, Mineral Baths, and Opera
House.   Garage adjoining.

AMUSEMENTS EVERY EVENING

DANCE EACH SATURDAY.
CONCERT EVERY SUNDAY.

G. W. BOSWORTH,

Tel. Address: "Comfortable."   Manager and Secretary.
Nat. Tel. No. 211 and 212.

Advertisment for the Buxton Hydro (circa 1910s)

Far more than some other spa towns, Buxton's medical reputation had always outweighed its attraction as a social resort. Medical treatises extolled the virtues of its waters, its clean air and healthy location. As the town developed as an inland resort and a national centre of excellence for hydrotherapy, innovations in medical treatments and investments in new medical facilities in the baths attached to the Crescent were necessary. This was partially to counter the rising popularity for opulent hydropathic hotels, or 'hydros', which were opening in Buxton. Malvern House Hydro (1866), Peak Hydro (1880), Haddon House Hydro (1883) and others opened to service the national growth of interest in therapies based on the use of cold mains water for its own sake rather than for any special thermal quality or mineral content.

To keep pace with changing consumer expectations and competition from other spas, it fell to the dukes of Devonshire, who were still responsible for the town's mineral water baths, to rebuild the Natural Baths and the Hot Baths. An initial rebuilding phase was complete by 1854, but a programme of internal alterations and improvements continued into the early–twentieth century. By this time, the Buxton Urban District Council had responsibility for the baths.

The result of this work was that, by 1909, over one hundred treatments were on offer, especially for rheumatism, gout, arthritis and tropical diseases. These included thermal plunge baths, douches (spraying water), needle baths (fine and powerful sprays), vapour baths, Turkish baths (communal steam rooms and hotter, dry heat rooms) and peat (or moor) baths. In peat baths, a signature treatment for Buxton, steam-heated peat and water were combined to form a pack which was applied to the body of the patient. After around twenty minutes, the patient was hosed down and wrapped in hot towels.

THIS IS THE WAY WE ARE TREATED, AS IF WE WERE GARDEN SHRUBS.

Engraving from 'The Water Cure Illustrated' (1870)

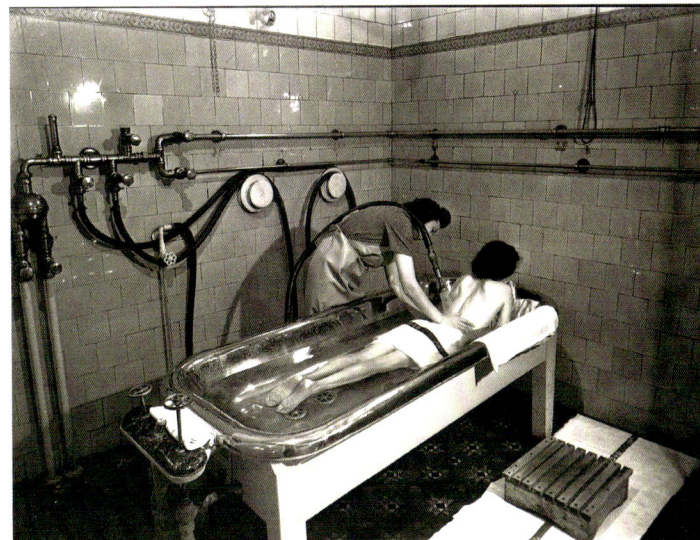

Patient receiving the Buxton Douche in the Natural Baths, The Crescent (circa 1940)

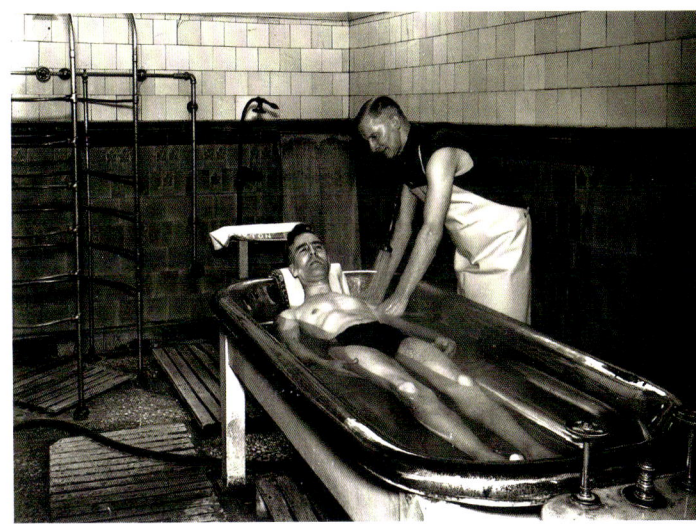

Mr Alf Martin, masseur at the Natural Baths Buxton Douche (circa 1940)

In front of the Crescent was St. Ann's Well. As elegant as John Carr's temple covering the well was, it offered little protection from Buxton's frequently inclement weather.

A new pump room opened in the Natural Baths in 1865 but there were complaints about charity patients thronging the Crescent arcade. In 1882, the separate Devonshire Hospital Drinking Well, for the use of charity patients, opened at the rear of the Crescent. This partly resolved the issue of overcrowding. In the 1890s, the decision was taken to build a new Pump Room in front of the Crescent. When it opened in 1894, its arcade and balustrade echoed the architecture of the Crescent.

St. Ann's Well – The Pump Room (1910s)

In 1912, the arcade was enclosed and an oval marble well installed from which water was ladled into glasses for public consumption. Although officially the building is called the 'St. Ann's Well', reflecting the fact that the water comes from a gravity-fed spring, it is still commonly referred to

as 'the Pump Room'. During the alterations, the stained glass window behind the oval pool was installed. It shows St. Ann in front of water-bearing rocks. The present external St. Ann's Well, next to the Pump Room, dates from 1940.

Interior of the Pump Room (1923)

Well attendants ladle water from the Pump Room's oval pool to serve to customers (circa 1920s)

By the 1970s, the Pump Room had become Buxton's Tourist Information Centre. Between 1981 and 1995, it was used as a 'micrarium' or 'museum of small things'. As part of the restoration of the Crescent complex, the Pump Room was refurbished as a Tourist Information Centre and a hub for the Buxton Crescent Visitor Experience and formally opened in June 2019. It is managed by the Buxton Crescent Heritage Trust.

Crowds gather for the opening of the Pump Room by the 8th Duke of Devonshire (1894)

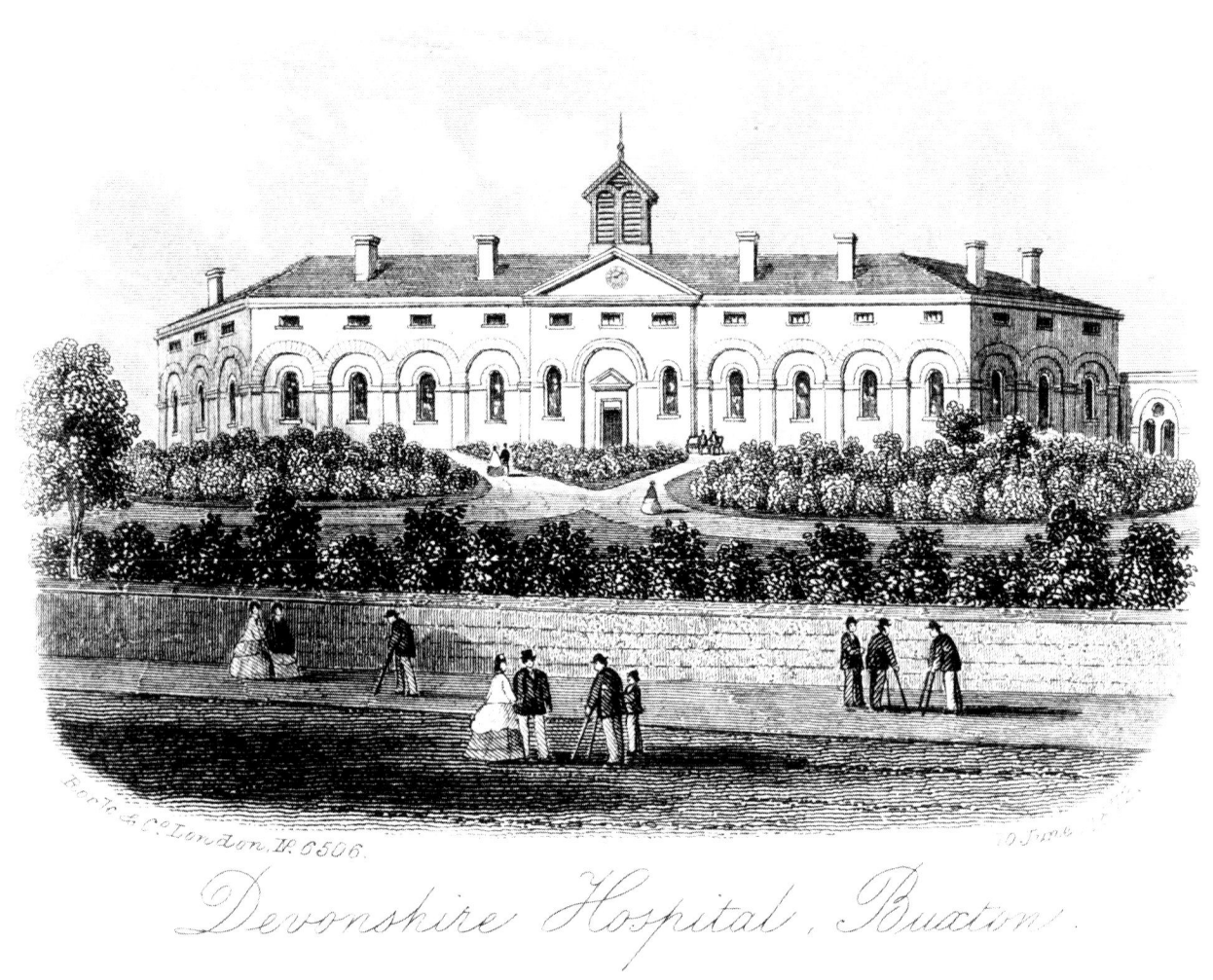

Devonshire Hospital before the dome was built (1872)

An essential development cementing Buxton's reputation as an inland health resort involved the conversion of the Great Stables into a hydropathic hospital. Part of the building had been converted in 1858. This was followed by the conversion of the remainder of the building between 1879 and 1881. Funded by the Buxton Bath Charity and the Lancashire Cotton Districts Convalescent Fund, the former central grazing area was covered over with a colossal dome. At over 145 feet (44m) in diameter, it was one of the biggest in the world. The hydropathic hospital, which later became the Devonshire Royal Hospital, was the largest in the country. It closed in 2000.

Hastened by the establishment of the National Health Service (NHS) in 1948, all of the UK's spas declined during the twentieth century.

This new service provided medical treatment free of charge at the point of delivery while, at the same time, largely failing to recognise the therapeutic benefits of mineral waters and hydrotherapy.

Interior of the Devonshire Hospital (1903)

An elevated view of the hospital looking north–west and probably taken from the upper floor or roof of The Crescent. The 'new baths' refer to the single storey block in front of the main hospital, added in 1913.

Could Buxton's water make you giddy?

William Henry Robertson MD, the doctor at the Devonshire Hospital in the 1850s and 60s, set out Rules for Drinking Water, writing, 'The waters are so fully charged with gas…apt to occasion some degree of giddiness of even headache, that it is prudent at first to drink the water by sips…'

THE CENTRE HOTEL AND LODGING HOUSES

The history of the central section of the Crescent exhibits greater commercial diversity than either the St. Ann's Hotel or the Great Hotel. Initially, let as lodging houses, in 1808 the central section became the Centre Hotel. Robert and Ann Smith were the proprietors. After Robert's death in 1821, Ann continued to run the hotel until 1828. Next came George Goodwin, son of the George Goodwin who had run the St. Ann's. Under his management, the Centre Hotel lasted less than a year. It reopened as a lodging house, but closed in 1830.

By 1834, William Shaw, the then proprietor of the Great Hotel had taken on the management of the lodging house.

In the 1840s, the centre of the Crescent housed a haberdashery shop run by Madam Percival, and a book and stationery shop which doubled as a post office and the office of the Buxton Herald. In 1848, the Promenade and Music Room contained a picture gallery, subscription newsroom and circulating library. From at least 1827 until 1870, Bright's petrifaction, marble, watch and clock shop occupied premises 'leading to the Promenade Room'. A lodging house in the centre was eventually incorporated into the St. Ann's Hotel.

St. Ann's Hotel, incorporating the Centre Hotel and lodging houses (1880s)

Selim Bright and Co. Ashford Black Marble jewellery set (1846–1884)

The Terrace and Hall Bank, seen from outside the centre of The Crescent (1860s)

BUXTON IN THE FIRST AND SECOND WORLD WARS

Healing the Wounds of War

Buxton's role in the First World War (1914–18) related to the Western Front in France and Belgium. Deaths and casualties were due to new weaponry causing devastating injuries. Treatment stations and hospitals close to the fighting areas were set up and special hospitals in England were established for the most seriously wounded. Buxton hosted two of the latter.

Soldiers being treated for Rheumatism, Sciatica, and allied diseases in the new Thermal Baths attached to the Devonshire Hospital. (1916)

In the Second World War (1939–45), injuries were similar but developments in blood transfusion, antibiotics and chemicals inhibiting diseases, such as DDT for malaria and typhus, were used in the field. Specialist treatments could be provided much closer to the fighting lines. Buxton's role in treating the injured during this war was, therefore, more limited.

Buxton's Hospital and Spa Facilities

In the First World War, a Canadian Red Cross Convalescent Hospital was set up in Buxton's Peak Hydropathic Hotel in 1916. A year later, this was absorbed into a more general casualty hospital evacuated to Buxton. This 'Granville Canadian Special Hospital' occupied the Buxton Hydropathic Hotel and four others, including the Palace and the Empire, the latter since demolished. The Devonshire Royal Hospital had 150 beds for Canadian patients when surgical and associated treatments were necessary. Around 100 soldiers a month were treated with traditional mineral water routines and the newer hydropathic treatments. Ambulant soldiers were encouraged to run the catering and administrative aspects of the Red Cross hospitals as part of their rehabilitation and initial occupational re-training. Those fit enough were able to enjoy the facilities of Buxton, with clubhouses and recreational activities being made available. After the war, the town's hospital and spa facilities aided the rehabilitation of veterans.

In the Second World War, the town's medical facilities focused on areas of specialisation that had emerged in the inter-war years. At the Devonshire Royal Hospital, these were orthopaedics and rheumatology. The town's water therapies had now been absorbed into a wider range of treatments. Gradually other mobility disorders and head injury specialisations were added, all benefiting both civilians and war veterans.

Buxton – a place of safety In the Second World War

Buxton was a quiet town, with an important secret role, providing large–scale, underground storage for bombs at nearby Harpur Hill. The RAF and civilian workforce in 'Maintenance Unit 28' reached 600. Many other groups also came to Buxton. They arrived from local cities facing intense bombardment and from Europe. Schools were transplanted from Belgium and Guernsey.

Commercial companies relocated to Buxton; Norwich Union Insurance occupied the Spa Hotel (later redeveloped as Hartington Gardens). The government department, HM Customs and Excise, occupied the Palace Hotel. A Jewish community was also established. Prisoners of war arrived too, suitable accommodation being set up in the Lismore area: they were said to be well treated by local people. With a few individual exceptions, these groups were made very welcome.

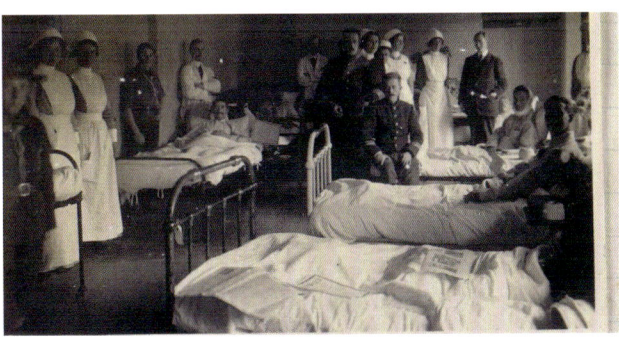

Photograph from Nancy Garnett's Scrapbook, Ward B, (1914-1915). Nancy was A V.A.D nurse, who worked at the Devonshire Hospital and the Canadian Special Red Cross Hospital.

In all, 656 Buxton residents and thirty–six allied servicemen, hospitalised in Buxton, died in both wars.

Above: Two photographs from Peace Day, The Crescent (July 1919)

THE CRESCENT IN THE TWENTIETH CENTURY

Decline and restoration

The Crescent Hotel closed in 1935. It was replaced first by the Buxton Clinic, a specialist rheumatism facility aimed at the middle class on restricted incomes. Later, it became part of Devonshire Royal Hospital, eventually closing in 1966. This part of the Crescent then remained empty for four years until Derbyshire County Council acquired it in 1970. After extensive renovations (1970–73), it reopened as council offices. The Assembly Rooms became a public library. Unfortunately, by the early-1990s, further structural problems were discovered and the council had no alternative other than to move out of the building and find a new location for the library.

The Pump Room and The Crescent (1973)

The St. Ann's Hotel continued as a family enterprise until it was sold in 1986 to a national chain. Decades of inadequate maintenance and a lack of serious investment resulted in the local authority having to serve public health notices on the new owners. Rather than addressing the state of the kitchens, the hotel was closed pending a full refurbishment scheme. This never materialised, and its 200-year history as a hotel ended in July 1989. Unfortunately, this part of the building quickly fell into serious decline as gales took off parts of its roof in February 1990 and water started to pour in.

The speed at which an empty historic building can deteriorate once it falls out of use is always a cause of great concern, especially when it is a Grade I listed building. It was evident to the local authorities and English Heritage (today known as Historic England) that the circumstances with the St. Ann's Hotel justified draconian intervention. Under the planning legislation, a listed building can be taken into public ownership if it is considered to be the only way of ensuring its proper preservation. As half of the Crescent was already owned by Derbyshire County Council, it was decided that the best way forward to save the entire building would be to bring the rest of it into public ownership. The local planning authority, High Peak Borough Council, did not have the resources to acquire the building as well as repair it.

The Royal Devonshire Hospital Annexe in the Crescent (1950s)

Instead, a case was made to central government, with the support of Historic England, that the Secretary of State should use default powers to intervene and provide the necessary funding to enable the urgent repairs to go ahead.

The approach proved to be successful. Following the Secretary of State's service of a draft compulsory purchase notice in 1993, the private owners entered discussions to sell by negotiation.

The National Heritage Memorial Fund provided the funds for the acquisition of the building by High Peak Borough Council, and Historic England was sanctioned to fund the full cost of the repairs via the largest grant, £1 million, that it had ever given for an individual building at the time.

It later granted a further £500,000 to Derbyshire County Council to complete the repairs of its end. The works to both ends of the Crescent were undertaken between 1994 and 1996.

Buxton's Public Library in the Assembly Rooms' Ball Room (1970s)

BUXTON CRESCENT AND THERMAL SPA PROJECT

Having completed the urgent repairs, the two councils acted seamlessly and embarked on a marketing campaign to invite proposals for the buildings.

Unfortunately, despite two attempts, very little interest was shown. Listed buildings carry considerable additional costs to refurbish and it was evident that, at this time, the local economy in Buxton was unable to support suitable schemes that were both viable and sensitive to the historic character of the buildings.

In the circumstances, an alternative arrangement was agreed and was to be known as the Buxton Crescent and Thermal Spa Project. Under this arrangement, the councils would enter into a partnership with a developer to create a more suitable scheme to convert the Crescent along with the adjacent disused Natural Baths and Pump Room. In the wider context, the hope was that a scheme could be prepared that would play a key role in regenerating Buxton as an international spa town destination.

The Crescent stands empty (1992)

Demolition of the former St. Ann's Hotel dining room in preparation for works to construct the new spa and hotel restaurant (2012)

A SPA FOR THE TWENTY-FIRST CENTURY

As it is not a protected or legally defined term, the public understanding of a 'spa' has widened in recent years to refer to a whole range of meanings; many large hotels market their swimming pools and fitness suites as spas as do the high street beauty salons, tanning salons and nail bars.

A spa, in the traditional sense, however, refers to a place where a range of treatments, specifically related to the individual qualities of a source of natural mineral water, is offered. The culture of spa treatments had largely disappeared in the UK following the establishment of the NHS in 1948. Despite attempts by the many spa towns to have their facilities recognised by the NHS for medical treatment, this was not to be.

The undercroft to the Natural Baths showing the wooden trucks on a rail system, prior to restoration. Called a 'Moor Bath', the trucks were filled with peat and hot mineral water and pushed into position for clients to step into from the floor above (2003)

On continental Europe and elsewhere, however, it continued to thrive long enough to capture the huge rise in demand for 'lifestyle' rather than the traditional 'medical', markets. Recent decades have seen a huge increase in demand from people who wish to take advantage of the therapeutic value of water for its own sake rather than as a treatment for a medical condition.

The potential for England's spas to enter into this new market was recognised by the city of Bath which was developing its own Thermae Spa project. The scheme was designed to spearhead the revival of natural mineral water spas in the UK and, after it opened in 2006, proved to be very successful.

Ensuite bathroom St. Ann's Hotel (2003)

The new project partnership for Buxton was advertised and resulted in the councils being able to work with a property developer with experience of working on complex historic buildings (the Trevor Osborne Property Group) and the owners of one of Europe's largest chains of spa hotels and resorts (CP Holdings Ltd, owners of Ensana Health Spa Hotels).

Together, the two businesses established Buxton Crescent Limited to deliver the scheme. Under the partnership arrangements, the newly created company was invited to prepare a scheme for approval by the councils. At the same time, the councils undertook to put together a package of grant aid to cover the exceptional costs of restoring the historic buildings. This public funding would sit alongside the commercial investment by the company to convert the buildings into new uses.

Upon completion of the building works, the councils would retain the freehold of the buildings but would grant a long lease to the company.

The agreed proposals involved an 81-bedroom quality hotel (5 star) linked to a state-of-the-art thermal mineral water spa in the Natural Baths, six shops, a visitor centre telling the story of Buxton's spa heritage and a landscaped setting to the buildings. A special feature of the hotel was its internal link to the Natural Baths to allow staying guests to have open access to the spa facilities. To maximise their accessibility, however, the baths would also function as a day spa, allowing anyone to book in for treatments.

Alterations to create new lift shafts, the Crescent (2016)

Staircase prior to restoration (2003)

These proposals were developed and submitted, first for planning approval, and then to the Heritage Lottery Fund (today known as the National Lottery Heritage Fund), Historic England and the East Midlands Development Agency for funding. All the approvals were successfully obtained and, by 2006, together with funding from the two councils and the commercial investment, the scheme looked to be ready to proceed. Unfortunately, at this point, some major problems developed which, if not resolved, threatened to jeopardise the entire project.

One of the main causes of delay in the project concerned its potential threat to the source of thermal mineral water given that the main spring is located underneath the Natural Baths which was to be converted into the spa.

Layers of wallpaper, St. Ann's Hotel, (2003)

The prospect of major construction works so close to the water source was a worry to all parties: the councils, Buxton Crescent Limited and the Buxton Mineral Water Company which bottled the water – as any damage, either polluting the water or adversely affecting its flow, would be catastrophic. The issue was only capable of being addressed by complex, three-way, legal negotiations to control how the works proceeded so as to minimise the risk. This took a considerable amount of time to resolve but, fortunately, the legal structure put into place allowed the works to proceed safely.

This delay took the project through the financial crisis of 2007–08 and the consequent round of public sector austerity measures. This, in turn, caused the banks to become nervous about their willingness to support the company and some of the public money promised for the project to be withdrawn. It also meant that, even after filling some of the funding gaps, the project was going out to tender during the period when the construction industry was catching up with itself following the financial crisis and when contractors were able to heavily 'price in' risk – something that was particularly expensive for this very high risk project. The partners had no other option but to return to the National Lottery Heritage Fund to ask for a significant grant increase. The lottery had already generously offered funding in 2006 but now, the loss of other sources of public funding together with the steeply rising cost of the project meant that the lottery was asked to nearly double its offer.

Fortunately, this was approved in 2014, much to the relief and gratitude of the rest of the project partners who, themselves, had also had to increase their investments. At the time of the increased offer, the Heritage Fund grant was their sixth largest ever offered.

Any restoration project involving a group of historic buildings will involve considerable risks as it is not until the buildings can be fully opened up that the extent of any physical deterioration of the fabric can be established. The Crescent and Thermal Spa Project proved to be no exception.

The Ladies Bath in the Natural Baths prior to its restoration, (2003)

Former public lounge, St. Ann's Hotel (2003)

Buxton Crescent Hotel, restored Thermal Pool (2021)

Darwin's Bar, Buxton Crescent Hotel (2021)

In particular, the former St. Ann's Hotel end of the Crescent was found to be in very poor structural condition. Although the building's original construction had been designed and the work executed to a high standard, it was the subsequent alterations, some from very early on in its history, that were problematic. Consequently, various parts of the building in the upper floors were found to have very little or no structural support following alterations at ground level and, in one instance, emergency internal scaffolding had to be introduced to prevent a major structural collapse.

The building contract, originally planned to last two years, ended up lasting over twice as long with the final four-month delay to completion being caused by the national lockdown in response to the global Coronavirus pandemic.

Notwithstanding all of these problems, the new hotel and thermal mineral water spa finally opened in September 2020.

Did You Know?

During the restoration, The Assembly Room's Ball Room ceiling had to be painstakingly repaired in areas due to water damage and then re-decorated. The floor had to be reinforced with steel beams and then the timber floorboards repaired and replaced with historic boards from elsewhere in the project. Finally, gaps in the floor had to be filled, boards sanded and many coats of varnish applied to bring the floor back to its original glory. Specialists were also brought in to restore the original chandeliers which had been boxed up since 1990 and the water damaged doors, which were then French polished.

The Crescent (2019)

THE EVOLUTION OF BUXTON WATER

St. Ann's Well in the summer (2024)

Did you know that the epic journey of Buxton's natural mineral water began as rain falling on the Peak District 5,000 years ago – around the same time as Stonehenge and the Egyptian pyramids were built?

It trickles downwards through tiny fractures in the rock, becoming purer as particles and microbes are filtered out. It absorbs minerals as it flows through the 350-million-year-old limestone. As it ventures closer to the Earth's core, it grows warmer and warmer. Until, at about 1 mile deep, another cycle of nature occurs: due to the difference in temperature, the warmer water at the bottom rushes upwards, pulling the cooler water at the top down, which itself becomes warmed and rises upwards in a circular flow system. The water must fight its way back to the surface, rising along a fault line – a hidden rift where the ancient limestone meets Namurian gritstone rock. Resiliently, overcoming obstacles as it pushes on upwards, it is still warm when it finally reaches the top.

Purified slowly, mineralised consistently, and heated naturally to 27.5°C, every drop is born of Buxton. This water could come from nowhere else. And, the spring is constantly replenished by rain, so the cycle never ends; today's rainfall over the Peak District will emerge from the spring in 5,000 years.

This natural spring first made its name as the 'Buxton water cure', believed to make the sick well again. Visitors travelled from far and wide to bathe and 'take the waters' and with the 5th Duke's improvements, Buxton developed as a fashionable spa town. Evidence suggests that by the 19th century, the waters were being bottled commercially to be carried beyond the borders of the town.

Today, BUXTON® natural mineral water is still quenching the thirst of people across the UK. It still flows freely from St. Ann's Well and is bottled locally by Nestlé Waters in a site powered by renewable electricity. The water comes from the same untouched artesian source, but the bottles have changed considerably – they are made with 100% recycled plastic (excluding caps and labels) and are recyclable at kerbside. Nestlé Waters works with partners and the local community to care for the water and its surrounding countryside to help protect and preserve this precious resource for future generations to enjoy. The team's work has been recognized internationally, achieving the prestigious Alliance for Water Stewardship Standard certification with platinum status – the highest rating available.

Buxton Water poster (2024)

BUXTON CRESCENT HERITAGE TRUST

Part of the case put before the National Heritage Lottery Fund regarding the bid for an increased grant was to improve the public access arrangements and to establish a separate charitable trust, the Buxton Crescent Heritage Trust, to manage them. The Trust was established in 2016 and opened the Pump Room as a tourist information centre in 2019 following its restoration by Buxton Crescent Limited.

One of the original attractions of promoting a hotel in the Crescent was that, it would allow more public access than, for example, a conversion into residential use. Paying guests can, of course, stay in the building and non–staying visitors can access the shops, bars and restaurants. It was considered that the fascinating story of Buxton's spa heritage, centred on the Crescent and spa buildings, however, was worth exploring more fully via a dedicated visitor centre. The Trust, therefore, designed and opened the Buxton Crescent Experience which is based in rooms on the ground floor and basement of the Crescent as well as the Pump Room.

In addition, the Trust manages a programme of heritage related events in the Crescent's Assembly Rooms by arrangement with the Crescent Hotel.

A visitor gazes up at a modern installation of Wedgwood cups and saucers in the Crescent Experience (2022)

A 'Mary Well Woman' school activity session on the Slopes (2022)

Our helpful BCHT team are always happy to share tourist information, the Pump Room (2024)

The Buxton Regency Ball, in the Crescent's Assembly Rooms (2024)

WALKING TOUR

This walk is approximately 1km long (0.6 miles) and can be completed in as little as 20 minutes. If you would like to pop into any of the wonderful shops, cafes, bars and restaurants on your way around allow more time.

The Pump Room

Starting at the Pump Room (SK17 6BH) step inside the Grade II listed building to see a place that offered both water and a fashionable place to relax and commune. Built in 1894 and substantially altered in 1912, it survived in its original use until the 1970s when the building was repurposed as Buxton's Tourist Information Centre. Another use for the Pump Room came about in 1981 when it opened as a micrarium, a place where microscopic organisms could be viewed under microscopes by an enthusiastic public.

Today, Buxton's Tourist Information Centre has returned to the Pump Room, providing information on great places to visit and experiences to enjoy in our town, the beautiful Peak District National Park and High Peak.

St. Ann's Well – detail on the Pump Room

While in the Pump Room you can find out more about this lovely historic building, indulge in some retail therapy in the gift shop, book tickets for the Buxton Crescent Experience and drink the famous thermal natural mineral water straight from its source.

The Crescent at Twilight

Outside of the Pump Room be awed by the magnificent Buxton Crescent Hotel. Completed in 1787 by architect John Carr on instruction of William Cavendish, the 5th Duke of Devonshire, this building originally housed two hotels. To the right the Great Hotel and on the left the St. Ann's Hotel. In the centre of the building were lodging houses and if you look up you will see the coat of arms of the Cavendish family.

Can you see?

... the antlers on the deer on the arms in the centre of the Crescent? These are real antlers of deer from Lyme Park near Stockport. They're far too intricate for stone masons to carve and have to be replaced every thirty years!

Pump Room Stained Glass Window depicting the Goddess Arnemetia

Cross the road into the covered walkway and turn left. You will pass old ghost signs telling us the former name of the hotel and the reception door for the current spa hotel. There is also a Georgian 'No Smoking' sign. The covered walkway ends at the entrance to the Natural Mineral Baths. Still in use today as a luxury spa, where you can swim in the mineral waters and enjoy many treatments.

If you have ever drunk a bottle of BUXTON mineral water, you will see from the label that the source is St. Ann's Well. Opposite the mineral baths the waters run freely. Join the queue, fill your bottle and enjoy! The current structure around the well was completed in the 1940s and each July is decorated by a colourful well dressing display, an ancient local tradition.

St. Ann's Hotel ghost sign

Natural Baths sign

St. Ann's Well in summer

Did you know?

The water you're drinking fell as rain 5000 years ago and has been underground ever since. It has been filtered by the limestone and picked up lots of minerals such as magnesium and calcium on its journey a mile deep where it is heated and comes back to the surface emerging still warm at 27.5C (82F).

Old Hall Hotel

Can you spot it?

Opposite the Old Hall Hotel at the bottom of Hall Bank is an interesting building. Note how every floor changes in design as you move up the building. Another ghost sign reveals the former use. Can you spot it?

With the Natural Mineral Baths on your right, walk towards the Pavilion Gardens passing the Old Hall Hotel. The Old Hall is one of England's oldest hotels and dates back to 1572–73. It is listed Grade II*. The New Hall (as it was known then) was built by the Earl and Countess of Shrewsbury on the foundations of an earlier inn or hostelry known as the Auld Hall. The Shrewsburys were custodians of Mary, Queen of Scots. The New Hall was built with the sanction of Queen Elizabeth I in the form of a fortified tower to enforce security measures for the Scottish queen when she was in residence. Queen Mary visited regularly and took the waters to provide relief from rheumatism. The New Hall was also visited by prominent members of the Elizabethan court including the earl of Leicester, the Earl of Pembroke, the Earl of Suffolk and Lord Burghley.

Still an hotel today, you can stay here or take a meal or drink in one of the bars and restaurants. Tourists are intrigued by seeing the window inside the building that is a copy of one which was apparently engraved by Mary Queen of Scots using a diamond ring.

Octagon Hall and Band Stand

The Buxton Opera House

At this point, feel free to take a detour into Pavilion Gardens. You will find a miniature railway, boating lake, play areas, cafes, shops and ice cream.

The gardens were enclosed and landscaped in 1871 by Edward Milner who started his career as an apprentice to Joseph Paxton, the head gardener at Chatsworth. He also designed the winter garden which originally comprised a Concert Hall flanked by two pavilions; the whole structure linked by corridors for promenading. The design was heavily influenced by Paxton's more famous Crystal Palace built for the Great Exhibition in Hyde Park in 1851. Even though there was a charge for entry for many years, the venture was such a success that the Octagon Hall, designed by Robert Rippon Duke was added in 1876. The Octagon proved to be a popular concert hall and in 1963 hosted the Beatles twice. It continues to be used for entertainment, fairs, auctions and other public events.

Resume the walking tour outside of the Grade II*–listed Opera House. This was designed by Frank Matcham and opened on 1 June 1903. Both interior and exterior are iconic with decoration ranging from Baroque Revival in the auditorium to the Art Nouveau glasswork in the foyer and on the stairs.

The cantilever design for the Dress and Upper Circles mean that there are no supporting pillars obstructing the view of the stage. It seats just over 900. The 1940s saw the theatre decline and it was eventually closed in 1976.

Auditorium of Buxton Opera House

After extensive renovations, it reopened in 1979. It hosts a variety of major events including the Buxton International Festival of Opera, Music and Literature and the Festival Fringe every July.

Another restoration took place in 2001 with the help of heritage lottery funding and today the magnificent building hosts 450 live performances each year, including drama, dance, comedy, children's shows, concerts, pantomime and opera. It also hosts the Fringe Theatre and runs community and education programmes. There are occasional tours of the Opera House, enquire at the box office, but the best way to experience this venue is by attending a performance.

Did you know?

If you have written a postcard while in Buxton, the Penfold post box opposite the Opera House is the perfect place post it. Designed in 1866 and listed Grade II, it is a rare large capacity model.

The back of the Crescent and the Devonshire Hospital Baths

Continue through another covered walkway along George Street. The George Mansions, originally an inn and then a hotel, became lodging houses and are decorated with another symbol attached to the Cavendish family above the door. Can you spot the entangled snake?

You're now behind the Buxton Crescent Hotel. Look up and to the right and you will see an outdoor rooftop swimming pool which is part of the spa complex.

Can you see?

From behind the Crescent, can you notice what is different to the front? The rear of the building has four floors while the front has three. Designed as a way to maximise space and profits in the building this is a very clever piece of architecture from John Carr.

The Old Courthouse is now home to several bars and restaurants previously the building has had many uses. The large room on the first floor was used as a Promenade room for exercise and for entertainment during bad weather before the Pavilion Gardens were built. It later served as a theatre, a concert hall, a meeting place for the Local Board (precursor to the Town Council), the Mechanics and Literary Institutes. But despite being called the Old Courthouse, save for a few inquests the building never actually served as a court!

Up and to your left is the magnificent Devonshire Dome. Like the Crescent, it was originally designed by John Carr of York as the Great Stables (with no dome) for the 5th Duke of Devonshire. Once the railways came to Buxton, there was little need for stabling and with part of the building already serving as a hospital by the 1850s, architect Robert Rippon Duke was appointed to design the dome and oversee a complete conversion to a hospital. Funded by the Buxton Bath Charity and the Lancashire Cotton Districts Convalescent Fund, the conversion began in September 1879 and the opening ceremony took place on 11 October 1881. Known as the Devonshire Hospital and, later, the Devonshire Royal Hospital, it continued to develop and flourish. New on-site mineral water baths were built on the lower land adjoining the south front of the hospital in 1914. During First World War, the hospital offered the War Office the use of 150 beds for sick and wounded soldiers.

Can you see?

Can you see the Grotesques on the building? These are thought to be from the 19th century and there are seventeen of them dotted inside and outside the Old Courthouse. They're all different – how many can you find? The word grotesque is derived from the Italian grottesca, which means 'of the grotto', so some of our grotesques are beautiful and not at all grotesque. Look out for more as you explore Buxton, there are more than 150 around the town.

The Devonshire Dome

Interior of the Devonshire Dome

In 1948, the hospital was absorbed into the NHS and ceased to be a charitable concern. It was managed by the South Manchester hospital authorities. It closed as a hospital in 2000. Following refurbishment, the building reopened to Higher and Further Education students of the University of Derby in 2003 and continues in educational usage. It has also been an established events venue seating up to 1000 dinner guests. Today, the baths remain in use as a fully operational day spa beneath the Dome and you can eat in the newly – opened Harpur's Bistro.

Can you see?

The Dome can be accessed by the public on certain days (usually during school holidays, some weekends and early evenings). Stand in the middle, clap your hands together and experience one of the strangest echoes in the UK!

Cafe life outside the Cavendish Arcade

Back on George Street behind the Crescent, proceed through a narrow gap between two buildings, turn right and right again through a large wooden door and into the Cavendish arcade. Now home to a wonderful range of independent retailers, the building occupies the site of the Buxton Hot Baths. The idea of warming Buxton's thermal waters to a higher temperature had been around since a notable physician, Dr Joseph Denman, proposed it in 1801. In 1816, the Devonshire Estate began constructing a complex of Hot Baths. They opened in May 1818.

By 1963, the demand for treatments had become so modest that the Hot Baths closed. They remained closed until 1986 when, threatened by demolition, they were saved by the Derbyshire Historic Buildings Trust which converted the baths into a shopping arcade.

Original Hot Baths tiling

Barrel vaulted stained glass roof

In the centre of the restored development you will see a 3000 sq. ft. (278.7 sq. m.) barrel-vaulted glass atrium designed by Brian Clarke. The glasswork, at the time of construction, was the largest stained-glass window in Great Britain.

Come out of the Cavendish Arcade through an alternative door you came in and to your right you will be able to see the starting point at the Pump Room or to the left Spring Gardens. At the top of the Slopes in front of you is the Market Place.

Did you know?

The beautiful tiles lining the walls were supplied by the Wedgwood company. They are still decorating the Cavendish Arcade while Wedgwood continues today as a famous ceramic company.

CUTAWAY ILLUSTRATION
OF THE CRESCENT

1 The Assembly Rooms' Ball Room

2 A grand bedroom in the hotel

3 The rooftop pool

4 The Pump Room

5 The Buxton Crescent Experience

6 Hotel suite

7 Cantilevered staircase

8 An attic bedroom in the hotel

9 The Assembly Rooms' Card Room

10 Coat of Arms of the Cavendish Family